THE SIMPLE VERSE: A DAILY RHYTHM FOR MODERN FAITH

THIS JOURNAL BELONGS TO

____

HOW TO USE THIS JOURNAL

You're here to grow, not to get bogged down by complicated systems. I created this space because I struggled to find a journal that balanced structure with enough room to actually breathe and think. This is designed to be a simple, daily rhythm for your faith journey.

THE DAILY RHYTHM: FOUR SIMPLE STEPS

Treat these four sections as a conversation with Scripture. You don't need to be a theologian; you just need to be honest.

1. **The Anchor** (The Verse):

Start by rooting yourself in truth. Flip to a random page in your Bible or pull up a "Verse of the Day" on a Bible app. Write it down here to set your focus.

2. **The Rewrite** (In Your Own Words):

Paraphrase the verse. Don't worry about formal language. Write it exactly how you would explain it to a friend. This ensures the truth moves from the page to your heart.

3. **The Application** (The Impact):

How does this verse hit home today? Whether it's a difficult conversation, a moment of stress, or a season of gratitude, write down how this specific truth applies to your current life.

4. **The Response** (Prayer & Notes):

Use the back of the page to talk back to God. Write a short prayer, a list of requests, or lingering thoughts about what you just learned.

A final note: There is no "right" way to do this. Some days your entries will be long; some days they will be short. What matters is that you showed up. I'm so proud of you for making this time for your faith. Let's get started.

"But let us who live in
the light be
clearheaded, protected
by the armor of faith
and love, and wearing
as our helmet the
confidence of our
salvation."

1 Thessalonians 5:8

TODAY'S DATE IS:_______________________________________

____
____
____
____
____

____
____
____
____

THE PRAYER

TODAY'S DATE IS:_____________________________________

THE VERSE

THE REWRITE

THE IMPACT

THE PRAYER

TODAY'S DATE IS:_______________________________

THE VERSE

THE REWRITE

____

____

____

____

____

THE IMPACT

____

____

____

____

THE PRAYER

TODAY'S DATE IS:_______________________________________

THE VERSE

THE REWRITE

____
____
____
____
____

THE IMPACT

____
____
____
____

THE PRAYER

TODAY'S DATE IS:______________________________

THE VERSE

THE REWRITE

____

____

____

____

____

THE IMPACT

____

____

____

TODAY'S DATE IS:____

THE VERSE

THE REWRITE

____

____

____

____

THE IMPACT

____

____

____

____

THE PRAYER

TODAY'S DATE IS:_______________________________

____
____
____
____
____

____
____
____

THE PRAYER

TODAY'S DATE IS:_______________________________

THE VERSE

THE REWRITE

THE IMPACT

THE PRAYER

TODAY'S DATE IS:_______________________________

THE REWRITE

____

____

____

____

____

THE IMPACT

____

____

____

____

THE PRAYER

TODAY'S DATE IS:_______________________________

THE VERSE

THE REWRITE

THE IMPACT

THE PRAYER

TODAY'S DATE IS:_______________________________________

THE VERSE

THE REWRITE

____

____

____

____

____

THE IMPACT

____

____

____

THE PRAYER

TODAY'S DATE IS:_______________________________________

THE VERSE

THE REWRITE

____

____

____

____

____

THE IMPACT

____

____

____

____

THE PRAYER

TODAY'S DATE IS:_______________________________

THE VERSE

THE REWRITE

THE IMPACT

THE PRAYER

TODAY'S DATE IS:_________________________________

THE VERSE

"

"

THE REWRITE

____

____

____

____

____

THE IMPACT

____

____

____

THE PRAYER

TODAY'S DATE IS:______________________________

THE REWRITE

____

____

____

____

____

THE IMPACT

____

____

____

____

THE PRAYER

TODAY'S DATE IS:____

____
____
____
____

____
____
____
____

THE PRAYER

TODAY'S DATE IS:_______________________________

THE VERSE

THE REWRITE

THE IMPACT

THE PRAYER

TODAY'S DATE IS:________________________________

THE VERSE

THE REWRITE

____

____

____

____

____

THE IMPACT

____

____

____

____

THE PRAYER

TODAY'S DATE IS:_______________________________

THE VERSE

THE REWRITE

THE IMPACT

THE PRAYER

TODAY'S DATE IS:_______________________________________

THE VERSE

THE REWRITE

____
____
____
____
____

THE IMPACT

____
____
____
____

THE PRAYER

THE VERSE

THE REWRITE

THE IMPACT

THE PRAYER

TODAY'S DATE IS:____

THE PRAYER

TODAY'S DATE IS:____

THE VERSE

THE REWRITE

____

____

____

____

____

THE IMPACT

____

____

____

____

THE PRAYER

TODAY'S DATE IS:_______________________________________

THE VERSE

THE REWRITE

____

____

____

____

____

THE IMPACT

____

____

____

____

THE PRAYER

TODAY'S DATE IS:_______________________________________

THE VERSE

THE REWRITE

____

____

____

____

____

THE IMPACT

____

____

____

____

THE PRAYER

TODAY'S DATE IS:_________________________________

THE VERSE

THE REWRITE

THE IMPACT

THE PRAYER

TODAY'S DATE IS:_______________________________________

THE VERSE

THE REWRITE

THE IMPACT

THE PRAYER

TODAY'S DATE IS:_______________________________

THE PRAYER

TODAY'S DATE IS:____

THE VERSE

THE REWRITE

____

____

____

____

____

THE IMPACT

____

____

____

____

THE PRAYER

TODAY'S DATE IS:_______________________________

THE VERSE

THE REWRITE

____

____

____

____

____

THE IMPACT

____

____

____

____

THE PRAYER

"May the lord bless you and protect you. May the lord smile on you and be gracious to you. May the lord show you his favor and give you his peace."

Numbers 6: 24-26

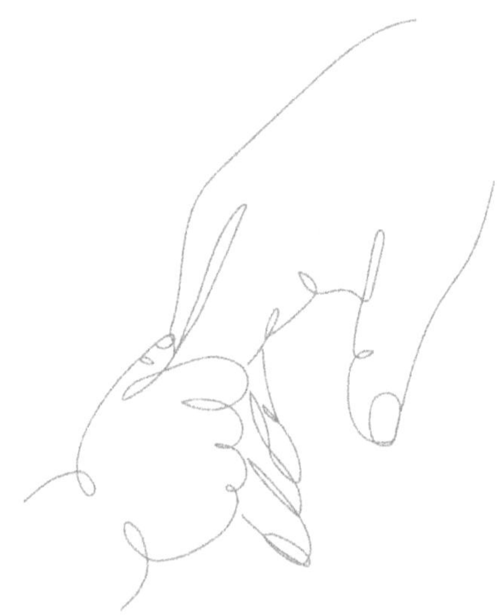

About the Author

Stephanie Stanley is a wife, mother, high school Spanish teacher, and the creator of The Simple Verse: A Daily Rhythm for Modern Faith. She lives in Omaha, Nebraska, where faith has been less of a tidy practice and more of a lifeline.

Stephanie is not a theologian or a pastor. She is someone who has sat in the hardest rooms life offers — and kept showing up anyway. Over the course of three years, she walked through miscarriage, a high-risk twin pregnancy, the premature birth of her sons, 105 days in the cardiac care unit at Children's Hospital Nebraska, and the death of her son Grant at eleven months old. She knows what it means to need a simple, honest place to meet God when you have nothing left.

This journal was born from that need.

Stephanie writes the way she prays — directly, warmly, and without pretense. She created The Simple Verse for anyone who wants a real faith practice but doesn't know where to start, or who has tried before and burned out. No complicated systems. No performance. Just a daily rhythm that meets you exactly where you are.

She attends Journey Church in Gretna, Nebraska, and is actively involved in the heart parent community and family support networks at Children's Hospital Nebraska.

9 798234 062239